W9-AER-153

What Am I?

A Hawai'i Animal Guessing Game

Written by Daniel Harrington

Illustrated by Susan Brandt

Mutual Publishing

Copyright © 2006 by Mutual Publishing, LLC

All rights reserved. No part of this book may be reproduced in any form
or any electronic or mechanical means, including information storage
and retrieval devices or systems, without prior written permission from the
publisher, except that brief passages may be quoted for reviews.

Library of Congress Cataloging-in-Publication Data

Harrington, Daniel.
  What am I? : a Hawai'i animal guessing game / written by Daniel
Harrington ; illustrated by Susan Brandt.
     p. cm.
  Summary: "A series of riddles and clues to guess the name of animal that
live in Hawaii"--Provided by publisher.
  ISBN-13: 978-1-56647-813-7 (hardcover : alk. paper)
  ISBN-10: 1-56647-813-8 (hardcover : alk. paper)
  1. Animals--Hawaii--Juvenile literature. I. Brandt, Susan, 1955- ill. II. Title.
QL49.H323 2006
591.9969--dc22
                                      2006023862

ISBN-10: 1-56647-813-8
ISBN-13: 978-1-56647-813-7

First Printing, October 2006
Second Printing, August 2008

Mutual Publishing, LLC
1215 Center Street, Suite 210
Honolulu, Hawai'i 96816
Ph: 808-732-1709 / Fax: 808-734-4094
Email: info@mutualpublishing.com
www.mutualpublishing.com

Printed in Taiwan

I have wings but I am not a bird.
My name is a common baseball word.
I like to hang upside down at night.
If you are alone I might give you a fright.

What am I?

I am a Native Hawaiian Bat.

I am one of the fastest fish in the sea,
And my nose is long and sharp as can be.
Yes, I am known for my pointed snout.
When you see it you might let out a shout.

What am I?

I am a Swordfish.

I am green, and I'm really quite small.
You may have seen me walk up walls.
Or across the ceiling upside down.
I am very small, but I make a loud sound.

What am I?

I am a Gecko.

I have blue blood, three hearts, and no bones.
If I lose an arm a new one will grow.
And I have no problem picking things up.
My arms are lined with suction cups.

What am I?

I swim in the ocean and dive deep down.
I sometimes make clicking and squeaking sounds.
When I jump from the water I spin in the air.
By the way, I don't have any hair.

What am I?

I am a Spinner Dolphin.

I look like an ancient pterodactyl in flight,
And my red throat pouch is quite a sight.
And just in case you haven't heard,
I am a native Hawaiian bird.

What am I?

I am a Frigatebird.

I walk sideways on the beach at night.
If people are near I hide out of sight.
But it is easy to tell just where I have been
Because I leave behind little piles of sand.

What am I?

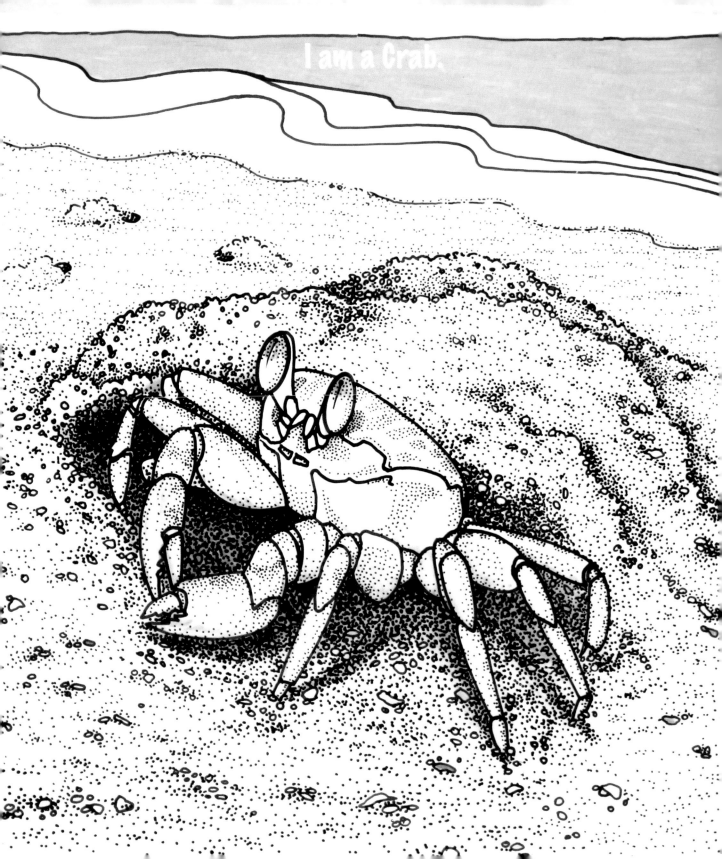

I am a Crab.

I have whiskers, and I am really quite round.
And I make a sort of barking sound.
I lay on the beach to sleep and rest
Because sleeping on the beach is the best!

What am I?

I am a Monk Seal.

I am long and thin and swim very fast.
By the time you see me I have already passed.
I hide in caves in the coral reef,
And when I open my mouth you see sharp teeth.

What am I?

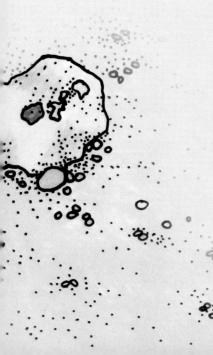

I am a Moray Eel.

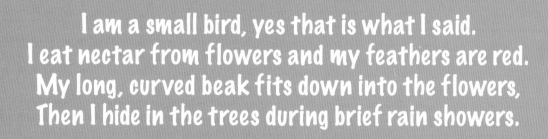

I am a small bird, yes that is what I said.
I eat nectar from flowers and my feathers are red.
My long, curved beak fits down into the flowers,
Then I hide in the trees during brief rain showers.

What am I?

I am
the ʻIʻiwi Bird.

My name is heavenly, and I like to swim.
My body is narrow and very thin.
And since I am a fish I also have fins.
Now if you can guess my name, you win!

What am I?

I am an Angelfish.

At night I soar silent through moonlit skies.
My body is brown, and I have two yellow eyes
That see well in the dark when I am looking for food,
Which I dive down and grab if it looks any good.

What am I?

I am a Pueo - The Hawaiian Owl.

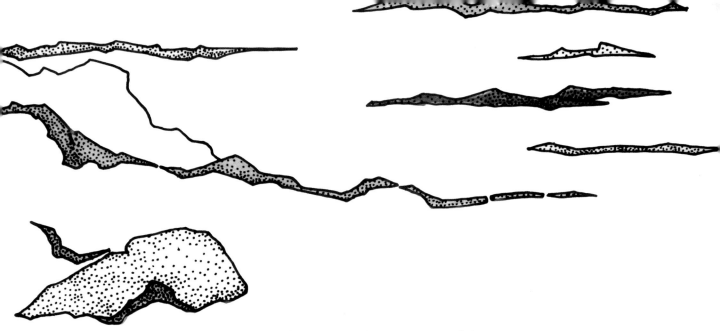

I am a friendly fish with a name like a bird,
And I help to make sand, haven't you heard?
I make sand by nibbling on coral reef.
To do this I use my very sharp teeth.

What am I?

I am a Parrotfish.

I have a wide, flat body and a wide, flat head,
And I flap my wings, yes that is what I said.
I soar through the sea underwater and then
I jump up above and then dive down again.

What am I?

Animal Answers

Native Hawaiian Bat

Swordfish

Gecko

Octopus

Spinner Dolphin

Frigatebird

Crab

Monk Seal

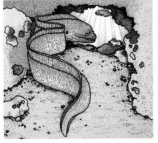

Moray Eel

'I'iwi Bird

Angelfish

Pueo – The
Hawaiian Owl

Parrotfish

Manta Ray

About the Author:

Daniel Harrington resides in Hanalei on the north shore of Kaua'i, Hawai'i. He is a teacher at Kula High and Intermediate School. Dan's hobbies are surfing and hiking, and he enjoys learning all about the Hawaiian Islands.

About the Illustrator:

Susan Brandt was born and raised in Hawai'i and received her art degree from the University of Hawai'i at Mānoa. Brandt worked at the Waikīkī Aquarium for ten years where she specialized in scientific illustration. Her work can be found in publications, exhibits and private collections.